BLACK FATHERHOOD:
Reclaiming Our Legacy

Dr. Curtis L. Ivery and Marcus Ivery

Interior designed by: Susi Cruz
Cover designed by Michael Short
Cover photo by: Blend Images
Courtesy of Shutterstock

It has been a pleasure and privilege to receive, love and raise my children, Angela and Marcus. I dedicate this book to them for giving my life purpose, meaning and joy.

Dr. Curtis L. Ivery

Table of Contents

FOREWORD

Of all the accolades and professional achievements I have realized in my life, there is nothing greater to me than being a father to my children. It is here that I have realized and witnessed the importance and impact of parenthood. It is also here that I recognize the missing pieces of our urban puzzles and the challenges that, as a result, plague our community.

The solutions we seek are not complicated, challenging, or hidden in a cave with a secret code needed to unlock them. They are simple, yet they are seemingly difficult to embrace and apply to our everyday lives.

Most importantly, they are rooted in parenthood—especially fatherhood, which is the perch from which I speak. Many other thought leaders share my opinion—that men must take a stand and step up to rebuild the black family—but not many have the platform from which to speak to the masses.

Dr. Curtis Ivery has used his role as chancellor of the Wayne County Community College District to impact lives and shape futures. He has shared his voice to encourage, inspire, and educate. He is now putting that voice to pen with an insightful view, shared by his son, on the need for strong fathers.

I not only applaud this effort, but also join in the chorus. We must all sing the same tune, and loudly, in order to penetrate the ears of those who are choosing or pretending to be deaf to the madness their absence creates.

— *Bill Cosby*

FOREWORD

Black fathers are caught in a crushing paradox: either we are the scapegoats for all that is wrong with the black family, or we are assigned magical powers in a cultural narrative of absentee paternity that suggests that if only the black father were present, black kids could overcome structural forces like poverty, racism and police brutality, removing the burden of societal reform from the culture that perpetuates inequality. That view, despite appearances, seeks to blame us more than praise us. What is needed instead is a mature view of black fatherhood that highlights the value of our presence in the lives of our families while helping us to combat the problems we confront. This book promises a rousing start to that effort.

Black Fatherhood is a practical handbook for understanding the multifaceted legacy of black fatherhood. We are the precious protectors and nurturers of our children, and, at our best, guardians of the sacred trust of partnership with our mates. We transmit the values of self-love, and love of our family and community, as we teach better by example than by precept or principle. Black fathers husband the moral and intellectual resources we possess to make something better of ourselves, and to make something greater of the world we inherit.

Black fathers also engage in daily rituals of self-maintenance that keep the self in order, even as we encourage healthy disciplines that keep kids on track. Black fathers fight against the seductions of patriarchal power and the exercise of brute strength, as we learn to share with our partners the ecstasies and disappointments of togetherness. Black fathers love beyond blood as they embrace children not of their own biological making, instead making them their own, and offering them care and affirmation that shape them more indelibly than DNA.

Black Fatherhood also contests the overexposure to media that exaggerates our weaknesses or ignores our strengths. Black fathers must battle vicious stereotypes of black male malaise while acknowledging the house cleaning we must do to offer our children healthy views of their bodies, minds and spirits. Popular culture offers tremendous opportunities for black youth to express their God-given talents, often in ways that challenge their elders' parochial visions of black identity. But there is something to be said for filtering the steady barrage of distorted images of black masculinity, and a pernicious diet of unhealthy beliefs about black female identity, that flood popular culture—and our pulpits and pews.

Black fathers must also come to grips with the truth that, as my late pastor and father figure Dr. Frederick G. Sampson advised me, we must love our children more than we despise our partners, once our relationship has run its course. Divorce and separation must not cloud our unconditional love for our children. Studies prove that non-residential black fathers spend just as much, if not more, time with their children than fathers of any other ethnic or racial group. That fact should dispel the myth of unloving and uncaring black fathers, though it doesn't mean that more of us shouldn't be even more vigilant about seeing, loving and rearing our children and being a redemptive presence in their lives.

Absence may make the heart of a romantic partner grow fonder, but it hurts the heart of a child in search of fatherly nurture. Even when a father is no longer physically living in the house, he may live vibrantly in the minds and hearts of his children through a vision of concern for their daily lives: how to peacefully resolve conflicts; how to tell the truth even when it hurts in the short term; how to relate to members of the opposite, or same, sex; and how to love reading so one can achieve an even more profound wisdom about one's existence.

Of course black fathers and families don't exist in a vacuum, but are shaped by profound shifts in our society. For instance, the shift from a manufacturing base to a service economy has deeply affected black families that haven't inherited wealth or educational privilege. These families must adapt to changing employment trends through retraining or skill migration. Black families that once depended upon manufacturing jobs to put food on the table and college in their children's future now face withering odds in an economy that sheds such jobs at an alarming rate.

Black fathers who once toiled in automobile or steel factories to propel their families up the ladder of mobility are now stuck on the lower rungs of economic opportunity, lessening the likelihood that their children will fare any better. Single working class or poor black mothers face overwhelming odds of rearing their children while seeking suitable employment to give them a better future. Those women, and poor black fathers, too, are often held accountable for their flourishing or floundering as we ignore broader economic factors that shape their life chances.

Then, too, our society has grown callous to the demands for racial justice. Black fathers are victims of a corrupt criminal justice system, police surveillance and brutality, and the vagaries of an employment scene where distrust of black men translates to severely curtailed opportunities. Racial disparities in the realm of higher education mean that black men, including young black fathers, are often on the short end of the stick: colleges and universities have poor strategies for retention, and often fail to successfully address holes in preparation that dog them from inadequate secondary schools.

Black fathers must perform their duties, pursue their dreams, and follow their desires in a world where racist views of black men persist, despite having one in the White House, and where compassion has dried up for the bruising barriers black men confront. Still, as *Black Fatherhood* argues, black fathers often do valiant work in the face of staggering odds, and it's that vibrant legacy of tenacity despite all impediments that make black fathers cultural soldier and heroes.

Black Fatherhood reflects the moral beauty, intellectual vigor, and spiritual maturity of the men who penned it. Dr. Curtis Ivery and his son Marcus Ivery are living the song they're singing. They exemplify the virtues of transmitting the values of black fatherhood from one generation to the next. The Ivery men work as a powerful tandem fueled by the desire to share their hard won wisdom with the world. *Black Fatherhood* is a bracing and uplifting call for black fathers to continue doing and being nurturers, protectors, and providers for our families. The Ivery men argue that we have a responsibility to love our families better and to surrender narrow views of what it means to be a black man and father. This brilliant father-and-son duo, and their literary love offering, is just what we need right now to fight stereotypes, build on healthy traditions, and extend the ethical arc of black fatherhood into this complicated but exciting century.

—*Michael Eric Dyson*

Nothing Is More Powerful than Words

Nothing is more powerful than words. When spoken, they can inform, educate and inspire. When written, they can guide, counsel, and encourage.

There are many words that continue to circulate about black fathers—they are not around; they don't care; they are non-existent. Those words—when paired with images of single mothers, struggling sons, and social ills—too often become what we believe to be our reality.

Our history shows us the value and impact of a father's presence and participation. Our present state shows us the impact of the lack of these things.

These words are the other reality—the reality of our purpose, our promise, and our potential to change the destiny of a culture. Thus, the reason for this book.

This book gives evidence and provides examples of what it takes to bind a family together, and make it work on every level. The effort is not without tribulation, but these words can minimize the trial.

The simplicity of a spoken word of encouragement to a child makes all the difference in the world. It means they matter, and knowing that they matter prepares them to be part of something bigger than they are—a family, a neighborhood, a community, and a culture.

The fiber of our family centers on strong character values—honesty, commitment, integrity. These are the basis upon which we grow, and help others to do the same. Our growth starts within, and these are the words to plant the seeds and nurture the garden for our children.

It is important that the words we hear, see, and read to resolve our challenges and strengthen our bonds take precedence over the ones we hear, see, and read that tell us we cannot.

What happens to us is up to us. We must regain control of our sanity, by starting with ourselves and our families. My every word reaches the eye or ear of someone in need of a push in the right direction, or an affirmation that he or she is already moving there.

If our words are our reality, may mine and my son's, as shared between these pages, become the blueprint by which we nurture a connectivity reminiscent of days passed but necessary for all of our days ahead.

—*Dr. Curtis L. Ivery*

A Father's Example Lasts for Life

My father is Curtis L. Ivery. He is also a husband, grandfather, educator, advocate, and role model, and is an inspiration to many. Yet his reach and impact go far beyond his professional, social and familial titles. More than anything, my father never abandoned his responsibility to me. In spite of what I now know was a demanding schedule, he always made it clear through his words and actions that we—I, my mother, and my sister—were a priority to him. His very presence helped to validate my importance by shaping how I saw him and how I saw myself. From the simplest of acts, like family dinner, fishing trips, or baseball games—where I played and he coached—the quality of our time together mattered.

My father is now the template I use to pattern being a father to my own son. He balanced a demanding professional career with raising a family. He never compromised his values or character; he chose truth over convenience; and he respected my mother and her contributions to our lives. He was and remains a role model, not just to me but to those who come into direct contact with him or observe him from a distance. He realizes that others are watching and that it is crucial to be a positive and productive example of what African American men can and should be. That's why the responsibility embodied in this book may in fact be the most important thing he's ever done—if it shows anyone else how to be the kind of father that our communities need and our children deserve.

As a young man, I naturally see many things quite differently than my father sees them. His childhood memories are unlike my own because we were raised in very different times and places. But we share a vision for the future because we have in common the same basic values that his father instilled in him and that he in turn passed on to me. These values are not antiquated, outdated, or even "just for old folks" as some would say. They are the basics of care, concern, and commitment that have held families together for centuries despite social and economic pressures that could have easily torn them apart.

In passing these values on to me, he gave me a connectivity that's largely missing today, because, somewhere along the line, that connection was broken. Stories were not told, dinners not shared, struggles not narrated. As a result, character and strength were not recognized and lessons were not learned.

Today, community leaders like my father are struggling to figure out "what happened" as they watch African American families fall apart and see too many young people wandering aimlessly through existence. Studies are commissioned and professionals are challenged to decipher what so many believe to be a secret answer to the struggles that envelop all of us. But the reality is actually as simple as family structure. It's about mothers being mothers instead of friends to their children, fathers being men, providers, and leaders, and the concept of community standing for something other than a sign on a recreation center. From this structure, respect is born, and character is bred. Children are nurtured, women are honored, and real men are made.

Whether it's a traditional family structure or a more modern variation, it is in the family that children are taught the importance of family and faith. They are told and then shown the way to a better life for themselves and those who will come to depend upon them. They know what obstacles to expect, as well as the rewards of success.

I look at my son and know, without being told or reminded, that I have a legacy to continue, not just a name to impart. It's the legacy of protection and preparation: protecting my son by preparing him for life's challenges and opportunities, preparing him by demonstrating what adult life is like.

It's a commitment to him but also to the community at large, fulfilled by making sure he is strong in mind, body, and spirit, and aware of his obligation to something greater than himself—our culture and humanity. Such protection and preparation are not to be found in a speech, study, news story, or rap song, but in the same places they have lain for centuries—the guiding hand and loving words of a father to his children.

—*Marcus Ivery*

The family is one of nature's masterpieces.

—*George Santayana*

Black Fathers Can Change Our World

Proud Family Histories— Gone Missing

As I look around, there is one clear void in our community of young black men and women: They know nothing about the enduring strength that resulted in their very existence today. Except for its occasional mention in history books or news clips commemorating Black History Month, this same strength is missing from the fabric of our everyday lives.

Too many young black men and women are living an unnecessary life of weakness and destructive influence. Negative images and behaviors overshadow the strength that fueled our ability to overcome man-made challenges designed to oppress and depress. These men and women are deprived of the opportunity to recognize the greatness that continues to run through their veins. So they never tap into this inherent trait, because they don't even know it exists.

Instead, their knowledge of history is limited, at best, to two or three figures chosen to define a legacy that cannot be confined to pages in books that few will ever read. They're much more likely to be influenced by video portrayals of contemporary men celebrating cash gained by any and every means, and of women flocking to these modern "providers," who have come to dominate the self-image of our culture.

The roles we African Americans—the unknown as well as the famous—once played in a world we helped to create are seldom present in the lives of those who would be better served by examples from the past. If they were, our youth would know of their ancestors' royal heritage, dignified behavior, and intellectual contributions. They would be inspired and would work to duplicate that level of respectability and honor. They wouldn't participate in or perpetuate the foolishness that creates and sustains stereotypes that overshadow what should be our reality.

Herein lies the value of story, lessons, and love from our elders. This is how true history is passed on—not just for awareness but for the template of how we should behave and continue to improve. We can't do either when the lessons and love are not evident or shared. Father to son, mentor to beginner, neighbor to neighbor, we need to know who we were so that our children are aware of what they're capable of and can avoid being anything less. The story is told, the lesson shared, and the love spread by what we tell, what we show, and the example we set. But who will start the conversation? Who will start the story for the rest so that they can turn the page? Either we recognize our past proudly and out loud, or we die as a culture and community, in silence.

My father used to play with my brother and me in the yard. Mother would come out and say, "You're tearing up the grass" "We're not raising grass." Dad would reply. "We're raising boys."

—Harmon Killebrew

Parenthood Redefines a Man—for Better—or Worse

No matter what parenting books you read or all the advice you might get from family and friends, nothing prepares you for the birth of a child. Becoming a parent is one of the most transformational moments in a man's life. It can be overwhelming to realize that the tiny baby in your hands is your responsibility to protect, nurture, and guide for all time to come. Simultaneously joyful and intimidating, it redefines the center of your existence.

Ready or not, the birth of a child expands your role as a man to something bigger and more important than anything else: fatherhood. Your child will wear the stamp of your being—forever. Your actions as a parent, good or bad, will indelibly influence his or her life. So it's important to make conscious decisions about how to love, encourage, and teach your children as extensions of your very heart and soul.

I was moved to write this book by my own positive experiences as a son and father as well as by my growing alarm at the widespread disintegration of the African American family, which poses a greater threat to our communities and culture than anything we've ever experienced since slavery. This is my call to all black fathers, that we spread the word about the significance in helping our children to be healthy, do their best, and, ultimately, contribute to the well-being of countless generations to come and of society as a whole.

I do believe that, deep in our very souls, we carry the imprint of those who went before us. Memories of the horrors of slavery; of the terrorism of lynchings and house-burnings after the Civil War; of and the legalized discrimination that ignited the social revolution of the 1960s and '70s are part of the way African Americans live in and see the world—regardless of when or where they were born. At the same time, however, we are imprinted with the legacy of quiet dignity, courage, persistence, resilience, and faith in the future, which characterized African Americans and their families during those traumatic times.

Dr. Martin Luther King, Jr. was strongly guided by a legacy of hope, courage, and faith as he led the civil rights movement through nonviolent protests and civil disobedience. In so doing, he uplifted the social conscience of an entire nation and, indeed, the world. Today, forty years after Dr. King's assassination, the mantle of leadership has passed to a new generation, and the dream lives on despite the worsening nightmare of what we've also become. The vision of a multicultural society based on the principles of equal opportunity, equal justice, and mutual respect is more real than ever before. But with so many black children now being born into fatherless homes, the dream can only be just that—a distant hope—for all of us.

Dr. King's gift stands before us, but we are not taking it.

Without Fathers, the Legacy Can Die

African American fathers play two critical and parallel roles in passing on a positive and hopeful legacy to future generations. We must nurture our children so that they enter adulthood with a foundation of universal virtues, and we must model the process of passing on a legacy so that they and their offspring can do the same. My own father modeled this process of passing on a legacy to me; this book, in turn, is part of my personal effort to do likewise, just as I trust that my two grown children will re-enact, reinterpret, and add their stamp to our legacy in raising their own children. In this way, we create a generational bridge over which the hard-earned lessons of the past are passed on to each succeeding generation.

Like many of his peers, my father was motivated by his faith that life could be better—not so much for himself, but for his children and for future generations. Through actions, much more than through words, he communicated his conviction that a good life was one of spiritual awareness, civility, hard work, patience, optimism, and loyalty. In a very real sense, his life was one of "walking toward the light." I do not mean to suggest that he was an angel; in fact, in some ways, he was a stern taskmaster. As children, we knew what the behavioral and ethical boundaries were. He set high standards for us, and he also modeled those standards. Even today, in conscious and unconscious ways, I am living according to the legacy he left. Especially when I am tempted to stray from his principles, I hear that still, small voice guiding me in the right direction.

If more African American men had experienced the benefits of a loving yet demanding father, our communities would not be in such crisis today. I hope, however, that the principles and examples in this book can help those who have experienced neglect, abuse, or abandonment as children find the strength to break this cycle of dysfunction as they raise their own children.

Otherwise, the absence of the black male in the paradigm of the family structure threatens the very role of the African American in society. What good is it to acclaim and take great pride in the past accomplishments of our people if the very nucleus of what holds us together is rotting at the core? Black culture is slowly being annihilated by an enemy from within. We are the problem, so we must recognize and face the truth before implementing a remedy—because we are also the solution.

A father is a man who expects his son to be as good a man as he meant to be.

—*Frank A. Clark*

What Went Wrong with Black Fatherhood?

Looking back, I cannot help but wonder where and how the black family became so disconnected. When did the separation begin? Society at large rightly admonishes our culture for its failures in this regard. And we admonish our young people as well.

We—as educational, ecumenical, political, business, and community leaders—must all step back and try to determine how we got here and why we continue to be mired, victims of our own self-defeat.

Was the culprit originally slavery? Economics? Segregation? Welfare? Or was it the overall evolution of a society structured to suppress black people? It has been said that slavery was a contributing or even the chief causal factor behind the breakdown of the black family. With fathers and children often sold off and permanently separated, slavery created a structure of female-headed households that some say remains evident to this date. Regardless, this only serves as an excuse to validate and condone daddy still being absent nearly 150 years after he was freed to be a man of his own destiny.

There is evidence that, somewhere along the way, black folks figured it out and made it work. The black family was once everything it was capable of being—strong, secure, productive, and dedicated to the well-being and future of the household. Similarly, limited education caused parents and children alike to value, respect and strive for higher learning. When the Great Migration from the South began in the early 1900s, many black men were among the two million who traveled to the North to find work for the benefit of families that initially stayed behind. This was not abandonment, but

The Media Tatters Black Culture

We can't talk about negative contributors to black culture without recognizing the unfortunate role of the media. Since the arrival of black people in this country, the iconography has been derogatory—and overwhelmingly influential. Advertising—beginning as early as the days of Aunt Jemima, with a rag tied like a scarf around her head, fueled the "mammy" image that many hold of black women today.

The foot-shuffling, weak, and subservient "Uncle Tom" has also been an inflammatory symbol of ignorance and prejudice since Harriet Beecher Stowe first published her novel in 1852. The caricature of irresponsibility, worthlessness, and absenteeism—remember the 1974 movie *Claudine*?—has long been at odds with the reality of more admirable black men and fathers. But have those negative images now regrettably become our reality?

Fast forward to today's overwhelming mass of instant electronic images promoting an ugliness that has become too much of our being and overshadows anything positive that we may be doing. What we're left with—or forced to see—are criminals, dropouts, and street thugs, all seemingly bent on mayhem and destruction. The success stories are unfortunately fewer, and typically less spectacular, than all the more outrageous tragedies and excesses we see around us in the media. This leaves little room to show the quieter fathers, businessmen, and educators who continue to be pillars of our community. Where are we if no one sees us?

Many may wonder if the difference even matters when it cannot be seen and measured. But I know it does, because we have the ability to begin the process of change.

All Men Are Examples, Good or Bad

Every man is a father, whether he has children of his own or not. He is a role model, even to those who appear not to be watching. So also can a fatherless child be influenced—for better or worse—by the words and actions of an unrelated older male.

This is why black men must step up to leadership roles within their neighborhoods, communities, and country, as well as in their homes. They don't have to hold public office or manage a major corporation to have a positive impact. They must simply always be conscious of how their conduct affects the manner in which they are perceived and, more importantly, imitated.

The principles of good relationships are the basis of all that we do. Interactions with other men, our wives, girlfriends, children, relatives, friends, and neighbors all serve as examples for others to see and learn from. This is how we can determine whether our communities will thrive or perish. They will thrive if we set high standards and live up to them.

What standards shall we choose to live by and pass on as our legacy? More than 70 percent of African American children are now being born into fatherless households. This has an especially adverse impact on black boys, who do much better in school, tend to avoid criminal activity, and are more likely to grow into productive members of society when they are raised in households with strong father figures. Yearning for how things used to be, or wishing to "go back in the day," won't change today's reality.

The vast majority of single black mothers do a truly heroic job of raising children on their own, but most would also readily admit that they could do better with a man's positive influence and presence. For more and more young black boys, mentoring is therefore the new "fatherhood" that fills the vacuum in their lives and serves as a viable solution to the perplexing social concern of fatherless homes.

"What they see is what they'll be," says Tom Wolford, president of the Detroit chapter of 100 Black Men of America, the national mentoring group that focuses on young African American males, "That is our philosophy." The businessman recalled the pride and joy he felt when a young student he was mentoring raised his grade-point average from 1.86 to 3.3. He said that seeing black men in positive situations—going to work and raising their families—reinforces the message that boys need to see and hear in order to avoid the kinds of behavior that put so many young men behind prison bars. "From exposing these young boys to job situations, work conditions, and sports, we help them see choices," he said. "The mentors spend time talking to them about what it means to be an African American male."

Kevin Hatcher, eighteen, is a younger mentor, but is equally enthusiastic about the role he plays in the lives of high-school students. Hatcher has deep respect for teachers, older neighbors, and others who have encouraged him. Because of their support, he plans to attend college. He's often complimented on being articulate, well-mannered, and responsible. He accepts the praise, but admits that he didn't do it alone.

"So many people helped me and shaped me," he said. "There are so many youngsters who are just as talented and special as me. They just need someone to help them. My mentors stayed on my case, and got after me when I made mistakes."

The potential for mentoring remains largely untapped despite its positive impact, according to Dan Mulhern, president of the Mentor Michigan program and husband of former Michigan governor Jennifer Granholm. "Every day, there are thousands of children whose lives could be dramatically improved if they had mentors," he said. "A mentor is simply a friend who can help you and an older adult that young people can rely on."

As an educator and father of two adult children, I have also developed an intense interest in the extent to which kids are influenced by strong father figures, whether they're mentors, stepfathers, or biological dads. Recently, several friends shared with me their childhood memories of fathers. Not all were happy; some, in fact, were very emotional and difficult. At the end of each recollection, the father's presence (or absence) proved to be the pivotal influence in their lives.

Without a doubt, the presence or absence of a father has a profound effect on the quality of life for black children. Those in single-parent families are one and a half to two times more likely to have behavioral or emotional problems than kids living with married parents.

No matter how one looks at it, the statistical big picture overwhelmingly suggests that we are losing the race.

As columnist William Raspberry recently wrote: "There is a crisis of unprecedented magnitude in the black community, one that goes to the very heart of its survival. The black family is failing."

Empty Bowls Beg to Be Filled

The Kids Need Your Example

Who can forget the image of Oliver, desperately hungry, asking for more bread and being cruelly shunned? This story, written more than a century ago, illustrates what our children need in order to thrive: love, guidance, and unwavering faith. As parents and community leaders, we need to embrace our children with a renewed vigor that will give them the courage to dream and prosper.

I've spent most of my life as a father, educator, and community leader talking and writing about this troublesome subject. But I am not a child psychologist, sociologist, or parenting specialist. I do not intend this book to be a parenting textbook or manual. Rather, I seek to provide practical and down-to-earth guidance based on my own experiences. I want to encourage and inspire African American fathers to live honorable, good, and truthful lives, and then pass on this positive value system to their children and future generations. I long to see productive, nurturing, loving families headed by parents who are overcoming great odds to raise great children.

At the same time, I despair at the irresponsibility of those who neglect the children they have fathered. Even so, I have written this book for them. I believe strongly in the inherent goodness of all people, just as I'm convinced that people have the amazing capacity to reinvent themselves.

I personally appreciate my own upbringing by a loving and demanding father. I rejoice when I see African American men in our city overcoming barriers such as low income and declining neighborhoods to still be great fathers, and I mourn others' abandonment of both home and community. As but one small example of what a tremendous difference fathers can make, a friend recently told me a story involving the theft of a small item by his ten-year-old son. Upon discovering the stolen item, the father brought his son back to the store to return the object and receive a warning from the store manager about the consequence of any such future actions. The father also withdrew certain privileges, such as television and computer time.

After these traumatic events, his son told him that he felt relieved of the deep guilt he experienced for doing something that he knew was wrong. This expression of guilt suggests to me that the father was on the right path. He was guiding his son in building a positive values system—a personal code of ethical conduct that will provide a moral compass for his son as he grows toward adulthood. As the son gets older, he will face harder ethical decisions, and his father will not always be there to guide him. He will need an internalized code of conduct when he is pressured to fit in with his peer group. He will need self-restraint when faced with the temptations of sexual activity, drugs, alcohol abuse, and aggressive behavior.

A Knock for Fathers

Knock at the door
Discover who's there
A man
In love with the sight, sound and scent of you.
Grateful to God for the blessings you bring

Knock at the door
And find
A provider
Who against the odds
Gives love abundantly; food, warmth and laughter; the seeds of full life

Knock at the door
And find
A servant
Daunted but filled with joy by you
Seeing you grow to be respectful, humble and secure enough to dare

Knock at the door
And find
A teacher
Helping you navigate myriad twists and turns
And to keep going, even when tired and afraid

Knock at the door
And find
Arms waiting
To embrace you after you fall
And encourage you to get up yet again

Knock at the door
And find a friend
As true as the north star
As constant as the sun
Made strong by unconditional love for you

—*Dr. Curtis L. Ivery*

Education is the most powerful weapon which you can use to change the world.

—Nelson Mandela

CHAPTER I

Black Fathers and Sons—
Leave a Legacy

I am not ashamed of my grandparents for having been slaves. I am only ashamed for having at one time been ashamed.

—Ralph Ellison

Pass the Torch

Lives are shaped by the hands that guide them, none bigger or stronger than those of an active father. Historically, black men have been the backbone of the family and community—the quiet strength relied upon and cherished by many. As husbands, fathers, caregivers and providers, countless men before us have been dedicated to a long tradition of determination and hope that forms who we all are today.

The father-child bond begins at birth and continues to grow throughout life. While the world around us has evolved in numerous ways, the simple and basic formula for paternal success remains the same; it is rooted in love. Fatherhood is an incomparable privilege and tremendous responsibility. Through shaping the character of another human being, fathering is the ongoing, lifelong act of designing, building, and leaving a legacy. It's important to think about what shapes our sons and daughters, and how it affects who they become. How do we use everyday experiences to help them do better? What lessons must they learn so that one day they will be able to continue strengthening our families and communities without us?

By example, the father demonstrates to his child how to become a caring and responsible person and parent. His actions and words directly effect the values that define his family, how his grandchildren will be raised, and the quality of life to be enjoyed by present and future generations. As time passes and his sons and daughters step up to the challenges of parenthood themselves, his bequest will be apparent and lessons shared in how they build on that legacy.

Single mothers know better than anyone what it's like to perpetually attempt to make up for an absent father. A mother's family role is irreplaceable, but so too is a father's. Parenthood is not a responsibility a mother should bear alone. Children need to know that there are reasons for a father's absence, but ever greater reasons for his presence. Nothing short of death should ever keep a father away from his children.

When a father is present, engagement, communication, and action become the keys to stronger futures through stronger children. Without such engagement, the character lessons of the past can be lost—and all the courage and sacrifice of our ancestors can be lost to future generations. To maintain this heritage, particularly in these critical times when it may be lost, it's important to remember who we are as black fathers and what our children, particularly our sons, are capable of becoming with our guidance. Everything else we own or do loses value if our children don't have happiness, well-being, self-respect, and reverence. The rewards of good parenting make all the effort as necessary as it is worthwhile.

So we must save our heritage. Practicing a tradition of stories and lessons perpetuates a heritage of strength and character. It emphasizes that for every action there is a reaction and that every effort the father makes will influence his child's life, now and forever. The sons and daughters we raise, nurture, and counsel will determine what endures and what new traditions will be created. When we leave the world, our children will carry the torch. Nothing is more profound than a father's teaching his son to be a man by positively supporting the cycle of fatherhood. In hopes of building on past victories, lessons of life and love are passed from one generation to the next. Becoming a father is an opportunity to re-evaluate who we are and what legacy we hope to leave through the everlasting imprint on our sons.

Many new fathers take full advantage of the opportunity to either pass on the traits and lessons from their own fathers or replace them with something better. They teach patience by being patient, love by loving, and honor by being honorable. In this way, they determine more than anyone else whether their sons inherit a blazing torch of leadership or are consumed by the flames of self-destruction.

Hard Work and Solid Values Leave a Lasting Imprint

Ask any good father about his obligation to his family, and his first response will probably have something to do with the drive to provide. This means working hard to make sure that both basic and complex needs are met. As providers, fathers become the role models children depend on—not just for material things, but for the example of a work ethic that will last a lifetime. Hard work is not merely laborious activity. It's also synonymous with being focused, dedicated, and committed to one's job.

When children see their father as a reliable worker and provider, they naturally adopt his behaviors. His model shapes their values as they watch his every move and learn from his routines, mannerisms, and interactions with others. By demonstrating responsibility, honesty, strength, dedication, and commitment in the workplace, fathers simultaneously help to guide their children at home, and thus earn something far more valuable than a paycheck: They build pride and earn respect for achieving excellence.

Teach—and Play—by Example

Many sons point to their fathers as their star role models. Adolescence is a particularly critical time to be so influential, because that's when dads provide a stabilizing presence and help mold their sons' characters through experiences that will form the backbone of manhood. Through his words and actions, a father models how to be respectful and considerate of others—with family members and elders as well as neighbors, strangers, and friends. He also teaches practical lessons such as how to tie a tie, throw a fastball, change a tire, or deal with bullies.

One of the most universal bonding experiences for fathers and sons is fishing. Sports are another. There's something special about having one's dad as a coach or even in the stands as a steady spectator and supporter. A one-on-one game of basketball, pitting father against son, fosters the physical part of their relationship. A victory for either side brings bragging rights until the next contest, while serving as a special rite of passage for the young boy, who learns first to play, then to compete and then, as he grows and matures, to invariably prevail, before finally going easy on the old man in the same way a father goes easy on his son earlier in life.

No matter how small or insignificant they might seem at the time, all such daily activities add up to the collection of memories a child will treasure later and draw upon when raising children of his own. A father should therefore not only strive to always set a good personal example, but take every opportunity to teach the long-term consequences of bad decisions as well. That's how a son learns precious lessons that no one else can impart in quite the same unforgettable way.

A father's voice of reason becomes a young man's voice of conscious when he's faced with tough choices.

—Dr. Curtis L. Ivery

A Son's Commitment to His Father

A Commitment to My Father

I thought of you today, Father
And a surge of feelings
Difficult to express
Surged within my heart

How busy the days seem
So much to do, it seems
That perhaps you don't know
How much I feel for you

I've grown to be a man
With children of my own
Understanding now
More about you, and you with me

Now I know
That joy can be bittersweet
Missing the touch of tiny hands
While celebrating new growth

And now I know
Strong arms can link together
One generation to the next
To protect and love
Our children

—*Dr. Curtis L. Ivery*

A Father's Counsel on Time

Take Time

Play
It is the secret to staying young

Read
With knowledge comes understanding

Laugh
It is the wellspring of happiness

Pray
It is your link to God

Love
And know that you are loved in return.

—*Dr. Curtis L. Ivery*

Dad Was from the Old School

The Old School taught
Its lessons well.
My father passed its lessons on to me
And instructed me to tell

Work hard every day
Don't wish for handouts
Seek dignity in work
And earn your pay

Know how to be tender
And know how to be tough
And know how to comfort
When life gets rough

The Old School says
That boys don't cry
But Daddy knew that sometimes
It's right to let a tear rise to your eye

Dad learned from the Old School
To respect what he had
He made his things last a long time
To provide for us with his last dime

Dad loved the freedom
In the African American way
He directed us towards opportunity
And guarded our freedoms every day

Dad was from the Old School
And I didn't appreciate it back then
But I'm grown up now
And see the lessons from back when

They've made me the man
That I am today
So thank you, Dad
For showing me that I can.

—*Dr. Curtis L. Ivery*

It's Not Easy

It's Never Easy

It's never easy
To make amends
To accept wisdom
And turn it into practice

It's never easy
To begin again
With what you have and nothing else
After life has knocked you down

It's never easy
To choose compassion and love
Over anger and frustration
When you are wronged

It's never easy
To think of others first
To be unselfish
Even when you have earned your share

It's never easy
To make the best of a little
And look to the future
For better things to come

It's never easy
To think through your actions
Before they become a hard reality
Of life
It's never easy
But remember that
The harder path
Is what will make you a man

—*Dr. Curtis L. Ivery*

Everything my mother and father did was designed to put me where I am today.

—Henry Louis Gates

Discipline: A Gift of Love

Providing discipline is a challenging but important and unavoidable responsibility. It's interesting to note that the word shares etymology with "disciple"—meaning one who leans on a spiritual leader's teachings. Parents are leaders as they continually mold the mental and moral character of their children through discipline, to help them gain self-control. Setting consistent, age-appropriate rules and limits creates a loving, nurturing environment for growth. Children feel safer when they know the rules and limitations. They recognize and respect boundaries in their own lives and in those of others.

Healthy discipline fosters good habits. It expresses loving concern, teaches caution, and serves purposes that are understandable to even the youngest minds. It acknowledges achievements and good choices so that children can gain more independence—which everyone naturally wants from an early age. Even in moments of conflict, parents and their children can still love and respect one another. Disagreements are part of the growing process.

If parents can use mistakes as learning opportunities, remain calm, and involve their kids in seeking ways to resolve problems, children will develop healthy decision-making skills. Taking the time to talk things through ensures that everyone better understands why a particular solution is best for all concerned. While they may seem difficult at the time, such lessons can—and often will—stick for life.

Give Your Children Self-Confidence Through Authority

Children are born with a natural curiosity that leads them to challenge facts and authority. This inquisitive nature helps them test their boundaries and make intelligent choices by weighing the pros and cons of the information they receive. Some adults presume that a child must show parents the utmost respect at all times. Yet they fail to see the value of showing the same consideration to their children in return.

Honor also goes both ways. Children who are valued and respected by their parents learn to extend these same courtesies to others, including authority figures, such as principals, teachers, police, or employers.

Psychologists warn, however, that children who never question parental authority are more likely to succumb to peer pressure and experiment with drugs, alcohol, and other destructive behaviors.

Such children are "outer directed" and take their behavioral cues, in too great a degree, from others—early on from their parents, later from their peers. Questioning and dialog within the family nurtures children who, later on, are more likely to question the validity of what they hear from their peers (and from authority figures and politicians). The goal is a questioning child and young adult—not one who is against all authority.

When youngsters lash out at their parents, sometimes it is out of frustration with their inability to articulate what they may really be feeling. Shouting in a fit of anger could even

Raise Readers and You'll Raise Achievers

Raising a child with books can broaden their horizons like nothing else. It stimulates the imagination and creates a space for parent and child to make discoveries together. It helps them develop new interests, learn new facts, and empathize with others. When you read together, it becomes a bonding experience remembered long after childhood.

A few simple techniques help raise readers:

Let Your Children See You Read

Children imitate their parents. If your youngsters see you curled up in your favorite chair with an absorbing book—in deep thought with Maya Angelou or James Baldwin, or pondering Walter Mosley—they'll be more inspired to read.

Read To Your Children

From birth through middle school, most children love to hear their parents read to them. It can be a short story in ten minutes or a whole book over several nights or even weeks. Sharing a story creates special bonding time and can be a great way to unwind at the end of a busy day.

Let your children read to you

As your children's reading skills develop, don't be surprised if you feel overwhelming pride and enjoyment during these sessions. Study their faces or follow the words on the pages as they read to you—it's a delightful shared experience.

CHAPTER III

Be a Father Each Day, Every Day

Stay Close to Your Kids, Every Day

Some of the best childhood memories are of times spent talking and playing with fathers. These moments allow kids to develop an abiding respect for parents and their parents' experiences. The more they talk together, the more children rely on dads for advice—not because of the parents' authority, but because the sincerity and freedom of their counsel leaves no doubt that they really care.

Frankly, it is quite hard to understand why all fathers aren't more willingly involved in the rearing of their children. For sure, being a father is demanding, stressful, and exhausting at times. It's well worth it, though, as the rewards can be immense—from the very first instant the window of opportunity of influencing a young mind opens at birth.

There are unforgettable moments when we are there from the start to respond to their cries, hold and hug, and help with their care: See them squirm and wail as they adjust to their new world. Experience the profoundest pleasure in watching them seem to pause from their discontent to listen to your voice, whispering of devotion and commitment. Children won't judge your worth as a father by what you give them in terms of food, clothing, shelter, and gifts. What they really want and need is love, time, and attention. These basic necessities sometimes require genuine effort and sacrifice, but should be given as freely as the love that comes so naturally with birth.

Dads are most effective when they provide discipline and security while encouraging their children to meet life's difficulties head-on. Our full participation is necessary for our children's healthy self-esteem, motivation, and hope.

Being a role model is not simple or easy, but necessary and it is—in fact—unavoidable. For better or worse, our offspring notice how we treat other people, spend our time and money, and handle the joys and pitfalls of life. We give them a template that is critical in molding their behavior and shaping their approach to everything that matters most—relationships, marriage, work, and school. Creating a family environment with limits assures moral and emotional stability.

It is much easier to become a father than to be one.

—*Kent Nerburn*

Enjoy the Ride—Stage by Stage

Each stage of family life, with its unlimited variations, requires patience, love, wisdom, understanding, and a deep desire and commitment to make it work. Couples must commit to weathering the stormy seas while still savoring calm waters—both are part of the ebb and flow of marriage. Staying together takes strength, commitment, and the firm resolve to be a family first.

The Beginning Years

Diapers, bottles, crying, sleepless nights, first steps, toddlers, potty training, and more—Babies all so wonderful and new at first. Yet heavy workloads and the quest for financial stability make it difficult to juggle the roles of parent, spouse, and breadwinner. At this stage, just keeping all the balls in the air is an admirable feat and more than good enough.

The School Years

When children start school, new challenges arise. They begin having experiences independent of their parents. They interact with peers who may offer good or bad influence. They encounter contradictions to what they've been taught at home. Some act defiantly to assert their individuality.

This is the time for setting new ground rules and doing various things together. Whether it's regular meals, weekly physical activities, supervised homework sessions, prayers, or movie nights, these designated activity periods give children opportunities to ask questions, discuss problems, and express their opinions. Such family time is essential for building values, maintaining strong connections, and establishing character.

Adolescence

From puberty to adulthood, children vacillate between acting like needy babies and insisting on being treated like emancipated grown-ups. It's a time of transition, confusion, tension, rebellion, and anger that can dominate some teens' lives. It's no easier for parents approaching middle age and experiencing their own transitions—during which they may question everything and may even feel the need for new personal and professional directions. Family—and family time—still grounds everyone, and provides a strong foundation from which all can grow.

The Empty Nest

While many parents look forward to this stage, others dread it, because a primary focus of their adult years suddenly vanishes from underneath them. However, if they've raised their children well—and can adjust to a house without shoes piled at the door or the screaming antics of energetic youth—parents can finally relax while developing new interests and hobbies. Relish this extended phase of watching children blossom into adults; it's the longest stage of all, an opportunity to fully enjoy the fruits of one's labor and love. And, if you're truly blessed, there might yet be babies all over again in the form of grandchildren soon enough.

**Time invested by a father in a child's
life turns to wisdom, guidance, stability,
integrity and conscientiousness over time.**

—Dr. Curtis L. Ivery

Show, Don't Just Tell

There are many things that can be done from afar—like voting, shopping online, talking on the phone, or communicating by e-mail. However, fathering is not one of them.

A generation ago, there seemed to be a clear and widespread acceptance that fathers should remain active in their children's lives regardless of whether they lived in the same home. Lifestyles have certainly changed since then, as many now feed their offspring empty promises with a long-handled spoon rather than doing whatever it takes to truly nourish them.

A child's well-being today depends as much as ever on fathers who stay physically, emotionally, and financially involved. Such involvement is an invaluable investment, with at least double the return of wisdom, guidance, correction, stability, and integrity when it comes from both parents instead of just one.

Parenting doesn't end with conception. Just as it takes two individuals to create a child, ideally, it takes two parents to raise one. Growing up in an environment where father and mother clearly respect and love one another establishes a strong family foundation. Their joint presence creates a healthy balance throughout a child's social and emotional development. Equally important, watching parents as partners demonstrates how strong relationships are built and sustained—on tolerance, trust, compassion, compromise, effort, and hard work.

An ideal home environment is one where family values are embedded in daily actions. Teaching morality and religion at home prepares children for a life of love, faith, outreach, tolerance, and compassion. Fathers are vital to this nurturing atmosphere. A solid, loving marriage provides children with a sense of security. It allows them to grow strong, follow their dreams, and reach goals that reflect well on everyone around them.

When children test limits, mothers and fathers become critical allies to one another—a united force in the handling of problem situations. As disciplinarians, they must work together to provide and enforce structure, rules, and consequences. Fathers contribute no less than half the authority that's necessary to effectuate discipline and mutual respect.

The beauty and lasting value of good parenting isn't always immediately apparent. But as children grow up, get married, and start their own families, expect to see those same values passed down to your grandchildren.

> **My father didn't tell me how to live; he lived, and let me watch him do it.**
>
> —*Clarence Budington Kelland*

Divorce: Maintain the Connection

The reality is that sometimes things just can't be worked out, and not everyone stays together. But divorce in itself need not destroy any parent-child relationship. Yes, kids usually derive significant advantage from growing up in two-parent homes. But the negative impact of separation can be minimal if both parents maintain an active presence in their children's lives. When parents separate or divorce in the United States, mothers keep custody of the children more than 90 percent of the time. Fathers who shortsightedly believe that their role is therefore limited to financial support, or eliminated altogether, are both holding out on their children and missing an irreplaceable opportunity. They are depriving themselves of the memories, experiences, and lessons only fathers can create and share with children. They miss out on helping to shape the lives that they've helped to create. Stress is usually highest around the immediate time of a divorce or separation. For about two years after any such drastic change in living arrangements, children are likely to have additional behavioral problems. This is particularly noticeable among boys under the age of five.

Children sometimes imagine that their own behavior caused their parents' breakup, though this is rarely true. It's not unusual for a child to be angry or grieve over the loss of time with the non-custodial parent. But hearing complaints or criticism between the two parents, or from one about the other, only further victimizes children by dragging them into the middle of adult disputes, thus increasing their negative or contradictory feelings. It is much better to maintain, at the very least, a polite and cordial relationship in front of them. Cooperation, rather than open hostility and resentment, works better in the long run for everyone.

Grandparents Stand In

Due to the death, economic difficulty, disability, divorce, or imprisonment of a parent, black grandparents are increasingly being called upon to raise their grandchildren. As surrogate parents, they can provide care and a wonderful sense of tradition. There are often many comforting and familiar similarities between grandparents and their adult children. However, the age factor is significant. Grandparents often do not have the energy to raise children or seek out fresh perspectives on parenting. Like the first time around, it can be downright exhausting at a point in life when many thought they could leave behind such responsibilities. Yet those taking on this monumental task are frequently the real modern heroes of the disintegrating African American family. For them, a primary challenge is supporting the development of strong self-esteem in grandchildren, given the loss of one or both parents.

Youngsters sometimes wonder what they did wrong to cause their parents to leave them with someone else. These heartbreaking feelings can be calmed by talking about positive attributes of their father or mother (the grandparents' child). Depending on the particular situation, having a parent maintain some contact by regularly visiting, writing, or calling can also let children know they're still loved and missed. Sharing pictures of parents and talking about memories can help children embrace and sustain traditions of their larger family despite the breakup of their own primary unit.

Not having one's father as an active parent sometimes causes young boys to become aggressive and hard to manage as they try to mask their sadness and anger. Make sure there's an opportunity to sort out such feelings. A search for respect and the need to prove oneself are often noticeable. Boys with good male role models, including a grandfather, learn more easily how to conduct themselves properly by understanding and managing those feelings. Sometimes it takes a whole village to raise a grandchild too, so enlist the help of other families, friends, teachers, and mentors.

A warm, nurturing, loving father produces a warm, nurturing, loving son.

—*Dr. Curtis L. Ivery*

Teach Your Kids to Deal with Conflict

There are different perspectives about dealing with conflict. With boys, this is particularly challenging. It is important that boys as well as girls learn how to get along well with others, but males in particular must be able to tactfully defend themselves in a world that can be violent and unfair.

If a bully picks a fight with your son, do you tell him to walk away or fight back? Although each response has value at times, we need, more than anything, to teach our kids to use less violence in relating to others. It's a difficult issue with potentially serious consequences, as homicide is the second-leading cause of death among teenagers in the United States. Accidental death (mostly involving motor vehicles) is number one, while suicide is third, partly because bullied teens are at risk of taking their own lives. The problem isn't just among boys. The number of girls involved in physical altercations at school is increasing steadily. Obviously, violence often aggravates problems rather than resolving them.

Each situation is unique, so parents need to be creative in helping youngsters understand that there is a variety of ways to handle any high-stress situation. Kids can learn to be assertive—meaning that they stand up for themselves but respect others' rights without being violent. Mediation is being used in many schools and courts to create structured opportunities to explore solutions to conflicts. This process works well in many cases.

Given how quickly and tragically such situations can otherwise escalate these days, the best advice for youngsters is to avoid confrontations altogether and seek trusted adult support before resorting to the losing proposition of self-defense or violence.

A Father's Influence: To Swear or Not?

A friend shared a lesson he learned from his father—his moral anchor in a world that provides increasingly few. First and foremost, he said, his father was a man of honor. Often, when he thought about what was right and wrong, his father's face would come to mind, and he would ask himself what his dad would do. For example, this young man often heard vulgar language but knew that it wasn't right. How did he know? A lot of his friends and other people in the neighborhood used curse words. However, he never heard his father employ profanity or tell an off-color joke. In deciding whether to use street language or that of his role model, he chose to follow his father's lead. By not swearing, the father instilled in his son a lasting lesson.

The behavior a dad models can be an essential ingredient for children's proper growth. What he does, they will too. What he values, they will regard as important. What he dismisses, they will also ignore. A man's most positive personality traits are usually closely linked to having had a warm, loving relationship with a strong, competent, and nurturing father.

Degrading language, off-color remarks, insensitive comments, and curse words from a father will give such language false validity and result in similar use by his children. But their absence speaks many more volumes. A father who can express himself without coarse or demeaning language shows strength, patience, and self-control— far more powerful influences against which even peer pressure can't compete.

Family Time Is Crucial—and It's Fun!

In spite of the busy demands on a father's life, he must always find time to spend with his family so as not to signal that they are secondary to other things in his life—his cell phone, his business associates, his meetings, or anything else.

Sometimes fathers get too caught up in the "fight for survival" mindset, the knowledge that making money is key to providing for their familes. But there is another resource just as important as food and shelter: time. Children must know that, yes, work is important, but so are they.

So turn off the television, telephone, and all other forms of distraction. Look your children in the eyes. Hear them when they speak. Hug them when they need to be hugged. Love them as only a father can, while you can.

Everything else in life is recoverable, except for time. Children grow up. Time passes. And opportunities are soon forever lost.

Make Sunday Family Day

Families view Sundays in different ways—as a day of reconciliation, an opportunity to finish one week or start a new one, a chance to sleep, or a day of relaxation, or a mini-vacation with friends and relatives away from the workweek altogether.

Others see Sunday strictly as the Lord's Day, when they reconnect spiritually in their respective houses of worship. It is a day of inner renewal and celebration of faith.

How Sundays are spent is of course a matter of personal choice. Having a family day of enjoyment is a good thing, and does not have to exclude religious activities or worship. The day can accommodate both family and faith, which are certainly one and the same in the eyes of God. Just know that taking time to reflect on both will instill the same values in your children's hearts for years to come.

CHAPTER IV

From a Child's Perspective

Active or Not, Dads Have an Impact

The mantra of the national mentoring and leadership organization 100 Black Men of America is "What they see is what they'll be." It is also a simple summation of the influence fathers have on their own—and on others'—children.

Men are vital to shaping young lives. Their absence doesn't absolve them of this fact and obligation. Doing little to nothing for one's children is the very definition of abandonment and neglect. It has serious consequences for their development, even if someone else is taking good care of them. In a child's eyes, a father is frequently the quiet giant—an enigma of sorts whose influence is sensed if not always recognized, but who has an impact beyond measure. Just as his presence is powerful, his absence can be devastating. His commitment may vary, depending on the role he chooses as a dad, but there can be no doubt that whatever he decides, his children will undoubtedly be affected.

Is he positive, supportive, and loving, or is he cold and distant? Either extreme influences cognitive and emotional development, because a father's actions—or inaction—become embedded in the template of a child's life. He can impart cues and clues on what to do and how to be. He can offer insights into how to develop skills and understand limitations. Who he is, what he says, and what he does or does not do will, to a great extent, determine what a child will ultimately become and pass on to his own children someday.

Remember the Not-So-Good Old Days

Once upon a time, the parents of today were in high school. They were spending time with friends, mooning over someone, playing sports, and juggling academics. There were teachers, tests, hormones, cafeteria encounters, dating, driving, and the universal fear of what would follow high school. A lot has changed since then, but not everything. When they reach high school, our children will face the same stressful challenges we faced (plus a few new ones). Recalling and sharing our own experiences can sometimes help support today's students through trying times.

Believe it or not, many kids say they would welcome the chance to talk over concerns with parents and to explore solutions in meaningful ways (without getting into an argument). Yet some parents fear the interaction, forgetting—or perhaps remembering too well—that they were once that age and in their children's shoes. Or perhaps they remember reaching out to parents who were unresponsive or angry.

Take a deep breath. Sit down with your teen. Listen and talk while encouraging them to do the same. Although you're the parent, keep in mind that you too were once a stressed-out adolescent. Think about how relatively unimportant issues seemed major then. Thoughtful questions tend to work better than telling someone what they should do. The most important objective, two-way communication, is a key to successful problem solving.

When the going gets tough, parents often do well to seek out counseling or advice from others with knowledge of the issues at hand. One word, one conversation, one issue at a time, are all good ways to make teenage stress more manageable for everyone involved. Remember how you once would have benefited?

When a father is missing from a child's life—there is a missing link to who they are; a hole into their view of where they've come from, and who they might be.

—*Dr. Curtis L. Ivery*

Absence Leaves a Void

Ask any young man with an absent father to describe his home life, and you will likely hear a story of disappointment, personal pain, and a specific emotional void. This is a tragedy of enormous proportions.

Boys without fathers grow up missing much-needed guidance. They may become overly aggressive because learning to manage and positively channel aggression is a critical rite of passage. Without a father's presence, that aggressiveness is often paired with sadness and anger, which too frequently fuel hurtful, impulsive, anti-social behavior. Often, the result is a young man with an unconcerned attitude towards school, work, home, family, and even himself.

Without the positive influence and guidance of a loving father, direction from others fills the void, sometimes with disastrous results. Destructive, illegal, and unrestricted behavior feeds our juvenile justice system, where the prevalence of disrespect and indifference only further reinforces and feeds upon itself.

There are many things that need to be embraced while growing up, and there are also many things to be avoided. Learning to effectively navigate life's path begins at home, helped along by the strong, positive influence of one's father.

Pass Down the Good, Skip the Bad

Fatherhood's legacy is a matter of what is shared, taught, and ultimately embraced from one generation to the next. This can and should include the passing on of personal hobbies, interests, philosophies, stories, rituals, and traditions. It should not, however, involve the inherited baggage of harmful emotions, stress, anger, abuse, indifference, or neglect from the past. These are heavy and unfair burdens for children to bear— negative traits to be removed from the evolutionary chain before getting handed down from another unfortunate generation to the next.

Although adult relationships—especially parental ones—can be complicated and will sometimes result in unfortunate behavior, every effort should be made to minimize the destructive outcomes adult problems can have on children. Youngsters naturally want to love both parents the same, so high-stress interactions between mom and dad often leave children feeling uncertain and uneasy in the middle.

Broken promises, arguments, or perpetual annoyance with one another are likely to affect young witnesses in many adverse ways. It is vital for both parents to be present physically and emotionally, treating each other with respect and compassion. Healthy relationships should be the goal of every parent, regardless of family dynamics or circumstances. Like everything else, positive expectations and guidelines help to shape not only the lives of children today, but can also affect countless future generations to come.

Be Their Rock

Nothing says stability and dependability like the combined parenting of a mother and father. Historically, this has proven to be a most powerful formula for equipping children with the tools they need to navigate to and through a successful life.

From education to social interactions, parents instill the values and practices that mold their children into positive and productive adults. When they see their parents working, and understand the ethic that goes with it, they learn the importance of providing for their familes and doing a good job at everything. When they witness loving interactions between parents, they learn about mutual respect, as well as how to show and receive affection.

From the simple act of discussing the day's events, to telling a story from childhood, a dad can show his kids how to relate to themselves and others. These connections create an atmosphere of care and stability—a rock-solid foundation for dealing with the endlessly diverse experiences that surround a child and the adult he or she will become.

Teaching Charity Can Change Lives

While giving usually starts at home, it shouldn't end there. Fathers can impress upon children the importance of addressing basic human needs, be they physical, emotional, or spiritual. They can also teach the value of supporting society by giving to others. When parents share with their children the significance of charity and contributing to social causes, they set a strong example and high standards. Giving is seldom a one-way street. In the circle of life, what goes around indeed comes around, as people often learn their own value as a result of what they've contributed to others. It's wonderful to see children grow as they help teach younger childred to read or to do something as simple as collect mittens for kids living in temporary shelters. Assisting others also helps them recognize and appreciate their own circumstances. While there are always some who are more fortunate, there are always those with less. They need and deserve your support, just as your children need to realize that everyone doesn't enjoy every bounty.

Givers can and have moved mountains—another vital life lesson. Historically, when people have contributed both time and effort to overcoming barriers in employment, education, housing, and public accommodations, their efforts have opened doors to expanded opportunities and a more just society for everyone. There are many causes today that need support from everyone able to commit any amount of time and/or money. The act of giving often paves a path upon which others can travel to a better life. It has been, and should continue to be, a part of our heritage, not only for the good of our families but for the betterment of our communities and culture as a whole.

Honoring Parents Who Serve

The well-known history of our country's forefathers should include those who are sometimes overlooked: our own fathers and grandfathers. Many African American men and women have dutifully served in this country's armed forces. That tradition of service continues today, and deserves to be recognized and respected at every opportunity. Military service is one of many ways African Americans have connected to a once foreign and hostile homeland. At the same time, it has had the side benefit of providing schooling and training that might not otherwise have been realized, especially for those who weren't previously college bound.

Being in the military sometimes requires parents to be away from their families. Fortunately, today's technology offers a lot more opportunities to communicate and stay in touch. Regular letters, phone calls, e-mails, and even video messaging are important to family connections and stability. Whenever possible, traveling or living together in other parts of the world are rich new experiences during a parent's tour of duty.

By serving both country and community, people in the military learn discipline, dedication, and specialized skills that build pride and honor. They deserve no less than the same honor in return, as the service they give to family and nation strengthens both as a result.

A Father's Love for an Impressionable Son

A Father's Gift

Standing on tip toe
With hands upstretched
His face alight
With love

I reach down to
Lift him up
And hold him close to me
I thank God

For the gift
Of words
He whispers in his sweet voice
That tells me all I need to know

About the man
I hoped to be
And the father
I am

Daddy,
He whispers,
I want to grow up
To be just like you.

—*Dr. Curtis L. Ivery*

If the World Copied You

Can one man
Make the world a better place?

Wipe the trouble away
With a swipe of his hand

Or make selfishness and envy fade
With the sound of his voice?

Can one man calm anger?
Or make hearts beat with compassion?

I believe so.

I've seen one man calm tears
Inspire laughter instead of fear

I've seen one man love with strength
And lead with integrity

Knowing what the world could do
to a good man
And being a good man anyway

I watched you, father, show me
That one man is enough to change

His children
His family, and the world.

—*Dr. Curtis L. Ivery*

Be a Positive Role Model

The pressures of black fatherhood are numerous and varied. Yet there's proof all around us that we can be very good at it.

A father is our first example of how to behave (or not) when it's our turn. After childhood, wider experiences affect the type of family man we become. Do we emulate the grandfather who told us stories of the past? Will we keep up the tradition of family gatherings to maintain those ties? Or will we allow negative images of black men as irresponsible fathers to define our reality?

Black fathers must prepare their sons to be tough in certain situations, humble in others, and always careful. They must point out obstacles black males face in an environment where they are often stereotyped and profiled, while helping them to understand their own value and worth. Being a good, strong black father is more than possible—it's critical. The greatest shame about the situation we're in today is that all it requires is active involvement, positive support, the right role models, and a desire from within to make it all right. Being a father is not easy. But failing to be a father because you believe it to be more difficult than it is—is tragic.

Learning to respect people of different cultures, religions and economic backgrounds begins by learning to honor and respect your own.

—Dr. Curtis L. Ivery

Absent Fathers Promote a Cycle of Poverty

Successful economies benefit from workers who have the necessary job skills and are trustworthy, reliable, charitable, compassionate, empathetic, and polite. A desire to learn and excel is also important. These characteristics often have their roots in the family, but affect entire cities if those families can't deliver educated, hard-working applicants. By not being responsible for their children, absent fathers are therefore a primary factor in the legacy of poverty that seems to have permanently settled into our urban landscape.

Like dominos lined up in an endless row, each missing dad tips onto others, causing them all to fall in rapid and predictable succession. When children generally lack a deep knowledge base, solid work ethic, self-discipline, and coping skills, it affects the entire community. Eventually, undereducated and unskilled young people fending for themselves often resort to destructive and illegal methods of acquiring what they think they somehow deserve or should have. In turn, their behavior has a domino effect on the community as a whole.

Fathers play a critical role in disrupting this trend. By exemplifying and teaching honesty, strength, dedication, and compassion, they establish a strong foundation for their children. They make it more likely that such behavior will be repeated on down the line by other young people, thus uplifting the whole rather than contributing to its decline.

Teach Your Kids Tolerance. They'll Need It to Succeed in Today's World.

With the Internet, cell phones, social networking, cable TV, satellites, and other modern technologies, instant communication is possible around the world. Coupled with our global marketplace, a universal connection is both accessible and necessary.

Other countries are doing everything they can to ensure that their youth become educated and prepared for the jobs of this new, so-called "flat world." To maintain a strong economy, children in the United States must be afforded the chance to discover and build their strengths and then apply them as competitive members of the global work force. We need core values to compete with other countries whose ambitions are overshadowing our own.

It stands to reason that, as our children become members of the global work force, they will be exposed to co-workers and friends from increasingly diverse backgrounds. They will also be exposed to an ever greater diversity of ideas.

For us all to succeed—and to foster innovation, embrace diversity, and be inspired to help each other out—the new global workforce must work together in an increasingly cooperative environment. to foster innovation, embrace diversity, and be inspired to help each other out. But we will only succeed if our young people develop a strong set of positive values to drive their aspirations and actions. One such value is tolerance, or an appreciation for diversity-embracing life lessons from around the world. Accepting diversity means teaching children to respect people of different cultures, religions, and economic backgrounds while honoring our own uniqueness. Parents' views often are passed down to children. When people are scorned for their race or religion, violence and conflict rule. A more tolerant attitude fosters peaceful coexistence. In today's economy, it can also mean the difference between economic prosperity and prolonged decline.

Pride in being a part of a unique culture comes from respect for a diversity of beliefs and cultures.

—*Dr. Curtis L. Ivery*

Look Inside to Find the Strength

The bestseller lists are always crowded with a multitude of self-help books, indicating a widespread and natural human desire to be better and more successful at just about everything we do or want to do. While there are many opinions about what has crippled our urban communities, it stands to reason that traditional values often helped us through difficult times in the past. People worked with neighbors and friends and through their churches to break down barriers to opportunity on many fronts—from education to employment. In other words, they used whatever tools and opportunities they could find that would enable them to succeed, and they shared them with others who were in the same struggle.

In the meantime, many well-intentioned efforts originally intended to be no more than transitional and temporary, such as welfare, have become permanent crutches, resulting in an entitlement mentality and a seemingly endless era of dependency. Rather than looking to themselves first, people now expect government to change their less-than-ideal circumstances. As a consequence, they've learned to always blame someone else for every poor condition or compromised circumstance in life.

Government can't manage or afford to correct such deeply entrenched social problems. Somehow, we must find the strength from within to reinvigorate the sense of reliance upon ourselves and the communities we once enjoyed.

Our historic lineage of self-sufficiency fostered a strength that has endured, even if it's been forgotten by so many. They may have learned not to recognize or tap into that strength, but it remains evident all around us. By taking greater initiative, being vigilant against violence, modeling a strong work ethic, and ensuring that our children get the best educations possible, we can throw down the crutches of artificial support and escape the trap of government handouts. These crucial first steps are powerful building blocks for creating a future that promotes the black community instead of making excuses for it.

Whatever the Fashion, Moms Shouldn't Go It Alone!

New York magazine recently did a story on the growing number of women who are seeking motherhood without a relationship. They are single, successful, self-sufficient, and tired of waiting for a suitable and willing mate as their biological clocks continue to tick. After searching in vain for a loving relationship, marriage, and the prospect of children, they're choosing a more direct—though probably not the best—route to motherhood: the nearest sperm bank and artificial insemination clinic.

Sure, men can contribute the seed of life, and science, plus a willing womb, can do the rest. Or can it? In a time when we so desperately see the repercussions of the disintegrating family unit all around us, this practice seems full of contradictions and peril.

Parenting is hard enough for couples, and doubly so for singles, whether they go it alone by choice or not. It is an immense emotional and financial obligation that can certainly take its toll on anyone. For the child's sake, any woman lacking the support of a stable relationship should think long and hard about the responsibilities of single parenthood. This includes anticipation of the many questions her child will invariably have about his or her origin as time goes by.

No matter their intentions or devotion, mothers can't be fathers, too. They simply can't, by definition or practice, impart to their children the same things—with the same resonance, authority, and nuance—that fathers can. Although giving birth is one of life's greatest urges and joys, single women should carefully deliberate on this route before proceeding alone—especially without male assistance on standby for children conceived and raised in such an unconventional and non-traditional ways.

This whole book—and many other more comprehensive schools of thought—is based on the fundamental premise that children do better with fathers in their lives. Any who think they may be the exception to this rule should think again before so willingly taking the unintended consequences upon themselves and the children who will be most affected.

Parenthood isn't a spectator sport— it requires a physical and emotional commitment by both parents for best results.

—Dr. Curtis L. Ivery

Father-Son Exchange Endures

There is no greater exchange than that between father and son. It can be a word, a smile, a look, a hug. It is the conduit of love, respect, and laughter. It is legacy. An exchange between father and son is the lifeblood that connects them and continues to have an impact beyond the years that life allows. It is spoken or unspoken, but is always evident whether they're together or apart, and follows them both wherever they may go.

Part Time Beats No Time

Fathers who are no longer in relationships with the mothers of their children are still fathers. Separating from the partner is never an acceptable excuse for doing the same with the child. Too many children have a relationship with only one parent. There are reconnections waiting to be made between kids and dads all across the country. Men must understand and accept the responsibility of fatherhood as a never-ending reality, regardless of the ongoing status of relationships between parents. Certainly, physical separation will limit the time available for kids, but there is no reason that the difficulties of living apart should stand in the way of quality time together with the child.

Let's applaud those men who make the effort to maintain their role as fathers, and hold them up as examples to those who don't. Maybe we do need to reluctantly adjust to the new reality of today by recognizing that even part-time parenting is better than none. But that doesn't mean we should settle for anything less than the absolute minimum of more fathers spending all the time they can to reconnect—and stay connected—with so many deserving young sons and daughters.

Talk to your child about popular culture's hazards often—yours is the voice they will hear when they are faced with tough choices.

—*Dr. Curtis L. Ivery*

Beat Back the Negative Side of Pop Culture

All around us, various forms of high-tech communication and entertainment are monopolizing much of the time young people might otherwise be spending on more constructive pursuits with parents, other family members and friends. Videos, the Internet, games, music, movies, television, and radio all influence values and behaviors. These devices are poor fillers for the voids created by the absence of parental involvement. In other cases, they take priority over more beneficial experiences. With adequate supervision, these influences can have limited roles and impact. Without such oversight, they become substitute guides shaping the lives, behaviors, beliefs, and practices of our children.

Kids coming home after school to empty houses are often drawn to video games as an easy form of escape and entertainment. Many games glorify violent, self-destructive behavior as an acceptable, even heroic, way of life. Players are rewarded with points and verbal encouragement for abusing women or engaging in theft or lethal combat. From middle school to graduation, most children will have listened to more than eleven thousand hours of music and spent twice as much time in front of a television as they have in the classroom. Parents can counteract these messages, sometimes using the same technology; there is also a tremendous amount of healthy information and entertainment available through the media.

Don't allow indecent, excessively violent, or destructive messages in your home. Talk with children about the impressions these media seek to create. Ask thoughtful questions about how the messages serve commercial interests without regard for their effect on society as a whole. Guide your children to alternative choices that present healthier perspectives more in keeping with those you care to uphold in your own life and household.

Help Kids Pull up Their Pants, and Their Self-Respect

In addition to looking sloppy, disrespectful, and just downright indecent, the practice of wearing one's pants below the behind may signal a much greater problem—lack of pride.

It reminds the better raised of how we learned as youngsters that a clean and orderly life does indeed literally start with a neat and tidy room. When we're in control and confident of our words and actions, this same control and confidence is evident in all other aspects of our presentation.

If that universal, clean-room principle still stands true, we can only conclude that a majority of our young men today are disconnected, insecure, and lost. They have no sense of being, and lack a level of pride that would otherwise make sagging pants as uncomfortable as sleeping on clutter.

It's as if their pants reflect the fatigue and apathy of their lives, unkempt with little promise or hope. The real shame is that, with just a little less effort than it takes to pull down the pants and walk around that way, they could also earn attention for being superior—neat, clean, and sharp, just like the young men they'd all do much better to emulate.

We need to lift them up—the pants as well as those wearing them—to better fit their higher potential. Like the sociopathic music, language, and behavior associated with them, these saggers project an "I don't care about me or you" attitude toward other young men and a world that already expects little or nothing from this self-voiding segment so critical to our future.

Unfortunately, many of the young men sporting this "call for help" fail to see any reason to be prideful or ashamed, they're so undereducated, disengaged, unemployed, and hopeless. Yet it is the duty of everyone to somehow restore the hope and change their direction. From being a good father to serving as a role model for others, every man has the special obligation of instilling and maintaining pride both in his immediate family and in the larger community. Women can do the same by demanding nothing less from all the males around them. But only men can serve as the example of standards that must never again be allowed to sag so low.

Wearing an attitude

There is only one chance to make a first impression, which does indeed count, and can make a world of difference. Fair or not, style of clothing says a lot about a person. Like most young people, black males tend to look to outside influences for cues on how to dress and act—be they from rappers, singers, professional athletes, or actors. The difference is that those who've achieved such fame and fortune can well afford to ignore convention: They don't have to worry about the consequences of showing up for job interviews looking like street clowns or gangsters. Instead, they use these images to define or promote their personal brand, even at the expense of those they influence.

Needless to say, black fathers are in a much better position to teach their children how to dress for success by wearing the right attitude. The competitiveness of today's corporate world demands that professionals both look and play at the top of their game—or even look and play at a higher level than others.

If kids still won't listen to their parents' fashion advice, help them observe how many conscientious and self-respecting athletes and entertainers do dress well even when they're not compelled to do so by team rules or contracts. Maybe they'll realize that our men can look stylish and still be "cool." At the very least, they should always be aware of what and who they're modeling themselves after.

The Kids Are Screaming for Help. Listen.

A screaming siren is a signal that someone is responding to a call for help. It clearly lets others know where there is a problem, that emergency aid is on the way—and it takes precedence over everything else. But what about the equally piercing, yet silent, screams of our youth? Who is racing to their rescue if not us?

Challenges can seem insurmountable to young people. Compelling new research has concluded that this is actually quite normal, given that the human brain isn't fully formed until the average age of twenty-five. This explains many things about the teenage condition, including their general inability to properly project into the future or adequately assess many risks. And now there are more temptations than ever in the form of easy money, drugs, and reckless behaviors that often lead to violence and self-destructive tendencies, even suicide. The toll on our children and communities is staggering. It's critical to recognize and heed early warning signs of these abnormal yet increasingly frequent developments before it's too late.

The first step is to listen. Pay attention to what children are saying—or not saying. Ask questions and reserve judgment. If the challenges or circumstances are bigger than the two of you, then be the parent and seek professional help.

The black community has spurned mental-health intervention for too long. Counseling has been viewed, not as a common source of help, but as something for "crazy" people or those with so much money that they can afford to pay a therapist to be their friend. People frequently advise each other to "handle their own business" in all matters, including mental illness. It's a good motto for the most part, but when it comes to this one, handling your own business is no more practical, wise, or appropriate than treating your own medical ailments. The reality is that at some point almost everybody will face emergencies that warrant professional intervention and guidance. It's best to call for help as soon as possible. Even without insurance to pay for it, free or low-cost services are usually available. Quite simply, when your child gives a call for help, don't ever hesitate to answer with all due haste and alarm.

> ## The traits you demonstrate are the traits your child will learn. Love, warmth and strength will create a loving, warm and strong child.
> *—Dr. Curtis L. Ivery*

CHAPTER VI

Reclaiming Black Fatherhood

No More Excuses

The black father used to be the center of our families, neighborhoods, and communities. His presence wasn't questioned or unusual. He was just there—right where he was supposed to be, doing what dads do. But somewhere along the line, black fathers started drifting outside the family, leaving all care and responsibility for their children to a wife, girlfriend, grandparent, or social agency. Those who stay now seem exceptional rather than normal. Some trace the cause of this phenomenon to slavery and the forced removal of black fathers from their families. Others say men who are nothing more than "breath and britches" to their children, as our elders once put it, are the result of poor expectations and economic factors. Some blame poverty and unemployment. Some blame federal programs, like the now discontinued Assistance to Families with Dependent Children (AFDC). Regardless, the issue now is how to reunite our families. Challenges have evolved over so many generations that the father's role must be entirely re-established— meaning that, in many cases, it must be learned and taught anew. We need to reclaim our families by accepting responsibility for the lives we bring into the world, as well as for those abandoned by others. Fatherhood is the ultimate calling for all men, to stand up for the sake of families that cannot be whole without us.

Make Yourself Whole— Experience the Joy

From the moment his child is born, a real man takes on the new identity of father. Each defines this role in his own unique way, but there is always one thing in common: Every father must understand that he's in it for life. To be a father means being a significant part of your child's life despite any obstacles, pain, or expense. It's by living through these challenges that the ultimate joy emerges—in small doses right from the start—your baby's first smile, the cooing, laughter, and recognition of you as Daddy. When your child takes a first step, lifts a spoon to eat, or says "Dada," the delight is beyond belief.

The role of father is a balancing act as parental responsibilities are juggled along with work, being a husband or partner, the business of life, social obligations, leisure activities, and economic constraints. Sounds like a hassle? Maybe so, but nobody ever said it would all be as fun and easy as the act of conception. For those who commit to doing the right thing, the underlying principles that produce a healthy child, from birth to adulthood, are something each father must establish based on his unique circumstances and values. At minimum, they're no more complicated than discipline, love, and an honor for the family unit—so that it can become part of the larger African American culture once again.

Be a Parent First, and a Friend Later

As children grow, they will choose their own friends, and probably have many of them. However, no one chooses their parents. So children must understand and respect that what a parent chooses for them is nonnegotiable, based not on friendship but on love, concern, and a commitment to what is best.

When children get older, some well-meaning parents naturally want to be their pals in the hope of opening lines of communication that allow will kids to be more trusting and comfortable. But seeking advice, approval, or adult-like conversation with children makes the more important duties of parenting, such as discipline and nurturing, more challenging if not downright impossible.

Parents who don't provide appropriate structure for their kids will abdicate that responsibility to other family members, teachers, principals, pastors, or coaches. If none of these manages to help teens learn reasonable limits, they end up in big trouble—on the streets or in the care of the police, courts, social workers, or foster parents. If that doesn't work, then it's on to juvenile detention and, eventually, prison or worse.

On the other hand, when children mature under the guidance of strict and loving parents, adult friendship blossoms, after they've grown and can rightfully respect it.

Savor each step—care for them as infants, protect them as toddlers, educate them as children, teach them healthy decision making as teens—and they will become young adults who welcome your deserved friendship soon enough.

Now is not the time for blame or complaints—they do nothing to help our children. Now is the time to act; to provide a strong sense of security with whatever is available to help our children grow up strong.

—*Dr. Curtis L. Ivery*

Don't Pass on the Hate

While the complexion of America continues to change, the realities of hatred and prejudices passed down through the generations remain. These often subtle social cracks are as American as anything else. Our sons must be aware of this as they learn to navigate a road of life fraught with hazards, from chuckholes to chasms.

Black men who are strong, intelligent, and competent have always been somewhat intimidating in certain sectors of society. They are considered a personal threat or dangerous to a system still largely structured to maintain the status quo.

"We shall overcome!" does not mean teaching prejudice in return or perpetuating unkind feelings we should all be working to eradicate. Rather, it means that we must teach our sons to embrace their own value and worth. These lessons can build confidence and resilience while minimizing the damage of those who do not behave with reasonable tolerance for people from different cultures. Despite advances in attitudes and civil rights, it takes a long time to change perceptions, prejudices, and biases. By standing up for themselves while respecting the rights of others, black fathers help both their sons and the evolution of society and demonstrate that life can and should be good and fair for everyone.

Be Your Daughter's Hero

Fathers often feel extra protective of their daughters, wanting to shelter them from the harsher realities of life. By having a strong relationship with fathers, daughters learn positive self-regard and how to have healthy relationships with others, especially men. This becomes particularly important in selecting a future spouse.

A dad helps create the image of an ideal man for his daughter. He shows her how to be a lady in the company of the opposite sex. He provides insight into the otherwise mysterious world of manhood, dispelling common myths, instilling reasonable caution, and inspiring healthy expectations. Feeling valued by him, she will be stronger and more confident around all men.

Children frequently model relationships based on how their parents treat one another. If the father is disrespectful to the mother and abusive toward her or the children, the daughter will become distrustful of men while more likely to accept bad behavior from them. On the other hand, if the father and mother are respectful and loving toward one another, children are more likely to expect and demand the same in their relationships with others.

Society still has double standards for boys and girls. We must prepare our daughters for a variety of roles by teaching them to be tough in certain situations yet humble in others, to be discerning and careful in their choices and actions. Help them become proud, caring, and capable professionals, wives, and mothers, and you'll have a lot less to worry about as your daughter encounters the challenges of young adulthood.

Provide An Education—It Unlocks the Good Life.

The story of the ditch-digger's daughters provides a valuable lesson about the central role of education. It is the tale of a father with five daughters, a laborer who valued schooling even though—or perhaps because—he had no formal education himself. As a result of his strong focus on academics and constant encouragement to achieve, each of his daughters became a successful physician.

Education is the key to a better life of more opportunities and comforts seldom afforded to the unschooled. In the story, when one daughter assumes a passive attitude toward learning, the father makes her clean toilets and floors, telling her that this is what she can expect for an occupation without education.

Too often, African Americans trivialize the importance of education and its impact on one's livelihood. As a result, too many children pass through ineffective urban educational systems without learning the minimal basics of reading, writing, and arithmetic. Eventually, they simply stop trying because it's so difficult and they don't have the prerequisite school or family support. They don't know how to make the most of their interests and talents, or how to set goals that are meaningful and achievable. In the end, they can't testify to the value of an education, because they have no idea what it means or entails.

Maybe that would change if they all had to dig endless holes for a living. Then perhaps parents, students, and communities would finally rise up en masse to revitalize an educational system that is failing our kids and passing them on to a world that has so little to offer them in return.

Stepdads, Step Up

Stepfathers comprise the fastest-growing group of fathers in America. Nearly 75 percent of divorced mothers remarry. Stepfathers are the pinch-hitters of optimism to fatherless homes, and should be commended for stepping up to the plate to serve as substitute dads out of love for their spouses and children alike.

The lives of stepdads are fraught with challenges, though. Some children view stepfathers as a chance to develop a strong relationship with someone who cares about them, while others show resentment almost immediately. There are numerous possible pitfalls that come with being a stepfather, and few clear rules or models to follow. Giving and expecting respect is a good place to start.

In this unfamiliar territory, stepfathers need to work with their new families to design their own unique roles, by making an effort to understand the experiences and expectations of the children involved. When done correctly, the rewards can be just as awesome as a biological father's.

With a strong sense of self and responsibility, all men can be many things to their children. Rise to the challenge; the role of the black father is expansive—provider, protector, guide, and guru. But always be a father first.

Be Someone Special—a Father

Fathers Are Special

A father knows
How everything works
And is the smartest man
You have ever known

A father always has
A few extra coins
And extra warmth in his face
And hands

A father shows you
The world
In all its big, exciting, scary, amazing
Wonder

A father makes you feel safe
When all the world
Feels like a place
You're not sure you can be

A father expects
So much from you
But only because
He knows all that you can do

A father
Is
And remains
The most special man in your life

—*Dr. Curtis L. Ivery*

Be a Positive Influence, in Family and Community

Being a good father has nothing to do with how much money you make, how many toys you buy, or how many exotic places you've visited. It's about having the time, integrity, consistency, commitment, energy, and willingness to make a difference in the life of your child. Each of these contributes to raising healthy kids who feel loved.

We must embrace the traditions and values that sustained our culture through much more oppressive times. Our ancestors were able to do it despite the many obstacles they had to overcome, and so can we, in much the same way—as parents upholding standards of honor, morality, and character for their children.

A father's influence is also evident in his relationships with extended family, friends and community. Your spiritual attitude toward your environment shows your connection to people and things that matter to you. Demonstrating love, faith, support, and care can create a cycle of growth—renewal, and hope—not just for your own children but for every child in your neighborhood.

Play the Odds, and Beat Them!

Against all odds, a good black father will rise to the challenge of being the best father possible. He will show strength in facing obstacles rather than weakness when opposed.

He will defy society's low expectations of him. Instead he will raise the bar, knowing that those who come next, beginning with his own son, will do the same. He will remember and tap into a legacy of strength, helping to build a responsible reputation for all fathers once again.

Against all odds, the exemplary black father will no longer look outside of himself for the definition of who he is or who he will become. Instead, he will look within. He will find his own identity and recognize those who have gone before him. He will see that his children are shaped by the strength of his past—when civil rights' struggles didn't fix everything but did create a somewhat more just society.

So it is against all remaining odds that black men still have but one good choice: to embrace their families and be superb fathers to all our children.

Help Love Move Through the Generations

To an older boy, it may seem mushy at some point to have a father always hugging or telling him that he's loved. But by then, it's already too late to feel anything more significant than the solid foundation of confidence that carries us through life. Never questioning their importance as a constant source of happiness and love makes children happy in return—even relatively so during those most difficult transition years of adolescence, when they may not always care to show, admit, or receive happiness and love.

Fathers who embrace their role as teachers instill lessons while allowing children to learn on their own. They're clear about expectations yet realistic toward mistakes. Teaching sons to learn enables the independence necessary for further growth and learning. It shows, by example, the value of character in discerning right from wrong and the importance of always choosing the one over the other.

It's no secret that parenthood is a trial by fire. Children come with no instructions except our instincts and others' examples. But they are truly the most amazing thing this world has to offer. Watching them grow from the first moment of pregnancy produces an indescribable feeling of pride and unconditional love. At birth, it's hard to imagine them ever doing anything that would make us mad, and it is easy to pre-forgive everything in advance. Later, when they do cross the line, firm but understanding guidance helps children understand that there are limits—and enables fathers to follow through on those first, nurturing moments.

While one generation invariably differs from the next in terms of personality, convention, and circumstances, the foundation of our upbringing becomes the most natural template for us as parents. If that template is based in strong family connectivity, and we're blessed to have had both parents involved in our lives, there's a greater likelihood that those same parents will someday bask in the light of a new generation. Like most grandparents, they'll also see it as a chance to keep illuminating the path by sharing and showing the very characteristics and values they instilled in us.

It Takes Families to Raise a Village

It has become a cliché to say that it takes a village to raise a child. While we shouldn't diminish the truth of this concept, it is important for us to remember that the best 'villages' are made up of healthy families. It is only a basis in at least some healthy families that allows a village—our community—to fulfill its true mission of helping to raise children.

In days past, the African American family and the African American 'village' had a good, mutually supportive relationship. A strong family structure was once the hallmark of African American culture and families were open to all who needed one. The community was the family, and everyone embraced to meet all challenges together.

This was especially true for children when all adults would correct any for doing wrong, thus establishing and enforcing a universal code of conduct that left no room for doubt or equivocation. Now, at a time when single-parent households are increasingly prevalent, most people don't even know their neighbors. This steady decline of the black American family has been blamed on everything, including economics, education, drugs, and other social problems, but only seems to keep getting worse as the list of possible reasons just gets longer and more complex.

The most compelling explanation is as simple as what's obviously missing from the picture: black fathers. The alienation, disengagement, and hopelessness of young African American males are evidenced by the high percentage who are high school dropouts, unemployed and in prison. Many are sons of absent fathers, too—and, of course, these fathers are as well. And so the cycle continues.

Even while rightly advocating for greater individual responsibility, the larger community must also take some responsibility for failing schools, the lack of job opportunities, deteriorating neighborhoods, poor public transportation, racial discrimination, and other factors that create seemingly endless and insurmountable barriers to individual initiative and success. Being an effective parent begins with a personal commitment to family as the core unit of society—but it also includes responsible commitment to making our communities better.

We express this commitment first by the way we conduct ourselves as fathers first, then secondly, as members of a greater society that owes its past and future to the equal presence of both genders.

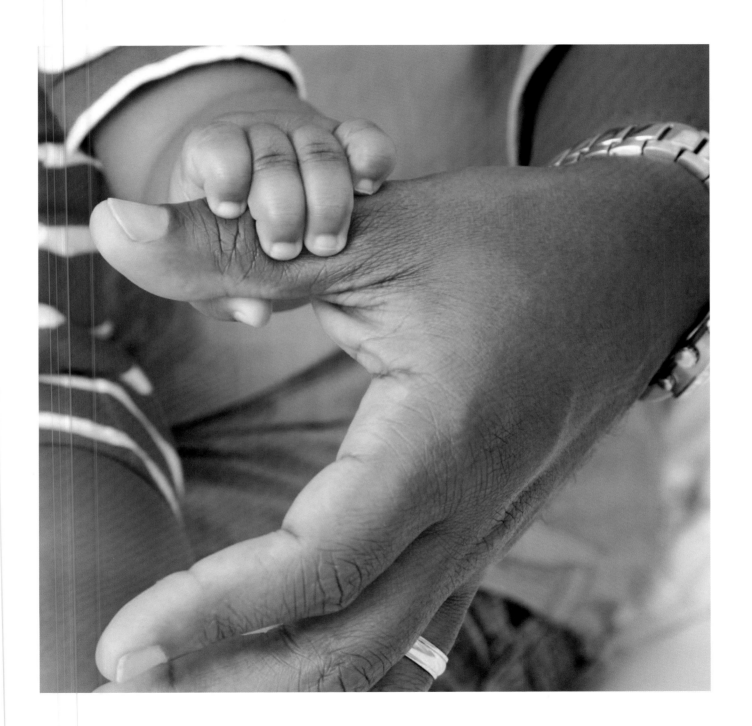

Reward healthy choices with love and praise. It teaches children that they are in control of making choices that improve their lives.

—*Dr. Curtis L. Ivery*

Continuing the Legacy

You've been given a priceless heritage. Pass it on.

To see a black father, son, and grandson all together at the same time would be cause enough for great pride even if it weren't so rare these days. When it does happen, they represent a lineage of undeniable strength and resilience built on a biological bond reinforced by the collective experience of social adversity.

Today's environment is vastly different from our fathers' and even more so than our grandfathers'. One generation grew up in an historically marginalized African American culture, while the very next came of age during a social revolution that demanded equal educational and economic opportunities for everyone. Today's beneficiaries of both experiences have witnessed more progress than ever before, despite the persistence of massive disparities between the races as well as between the rich and poor.

Symbols of progress are nowhere more evident than in the election—then re-election—of Barack Obama as the first African American president, and the recent dedication of the Martin Luther King, Jr., National Memorial, the first tribute to an African American and non-president on the National Mall in Washington, DC. And yet, in alarming contrast to these promising steps toward a multi-racial democracy, we still have persistent patterns of social division, inequalities, perceptions of white superiority, and mistrust between the races.

Throughout inner-city and urban areas such as Detroit and New Orleans, a high concentration of African American families is still marginalized by debilitating poverty, unemployment, inadequate education, and mass incarceration. A number of American cities are in fact in a period of re-segregation caused by the out-migration of both white and black middle-class families, leaving behind a poor, disenfranchised culture of hopelessness and separation.

Even as these images of promise and despair contradict each other, hope for our future lies in the same generation, of today's twenty- and thirty-somethings who are also the cause for so much concern. Despite the shortcomings of some, they are the most ethnically diverse, electronically interconnected, best educated, and politically progressive young adults in history. They are part of a generational shift back from the suburbs to urban areas where they're embracing entrepreneurship, multiculturalism, the arts and culture, livability, and quality education.

They represent our best hope for real change. Unshackled by social norms of the past, they will become community leaders of the future, and bring to this task youthful energy and enthusiasm coupled with a commitment to renewal rooted in strong familial ties. This of course requires African American males to recognize their special responsibility in support of all children and families, especially those living in difficult circumstances.

It is up to strong, visible fathers to keep serving as role models. We must encourage the brethren to counter the bombardment of negative and stereotypical messages with positive ones that do exist. Our conversations must focus, not on excuses, but on encouraging and guiding our men to assume, and retain, their rightful role as leaders, fathers, and mentors. We must show them that they are capable of becoming who we need them to be.

Fatherhood is evidence of a man's biological attributes, but being a great father is defined by character. Dads nurture and guide their children to navigate a challenging world. Regardless of family circumstances, real men and fathers are determined by who they are to their children. Love of family is the cornerstone of their lives, and being a great father includes giving unselfishly.

Building on the foundation laid by grandfathers, fathers, and external leaders, today's young men must face squarely the inequalities of race, move past the influence of a so-called "color-blind" ideology and "post-racial" views, and continue working towards a true multi-racial democracy. Obstacles do indeed still remain, but so does the opportunity to reach the next horizon of justice for our families and fellow African Americans. This dual sense of dealing with the challenges and realities of life while working to change them for the better has been the chief strength of black Americans for generations. It enables us to keep elevating ourselves to higher levels, with thanks and love to all the dads who brought us this far, and to those who will take us further.

CHAPTER VII

A Twelve-Step Step-Up Program for Currently Absent Dads

1. Realize that you are part of a proud African American heritage of achievement despite discrimination and violence.

2. Realize that, when you become a parent, like it or not you have become part of a long, honorable line of African and African American parents.

3. Realize that there are forces at work in the contemporary world that try to undermine your place in this proud history.

4. Realize that not all of your friends and relatives have the ability to think things through. So resist those negative influences.

5. Realize that fatherhood forces you to make decisions that will once and for all determine whether you are part of the problem or part of the solution.

6. Realize that your decisions define you as a blind follower of the easiest path or a thinking man who charts his own destiny and that of his children.

7. Realize that, whether you know it or not, you have a values system—the things you consider important. Realize that, more than anything that went before, the way you parent will show what that values system is.

8. Realize that, from time immemorial, the African American community—like all communities—has been divided between those who selfishly and foolishly chase the instant pleasure of the moment, or falsely posture for hollow honor, and those who think, plan, and succeed.

9. Realize that thinking, planning, and succeeding are more difficult than bowingdown to instant pleasure and your peer group—but that only through thinking, planning, succeeding, and doing what's right for your children can you achieve true happiness.

10. Realize that, although your peer group may influence you to be less than your true self, you can rely on more successful mentors—black and white—and on your proud African American history—to help you resist peer pressure and become your true self.

11. Realize that there are many excuses—slavery, emancipation, Jim Crow, segregation, desegregation, pop culture, the media, unemployment, underemployment, lack of opportunity—that are real obstacles. But they are not real excuses—and that, ultimately, if you determine to succeed, ask for help, and work hard, you can do the right thing for yourself and your children.

12. Promise yourself to take action: Become a thinking, self-directing person who can resist the current culture, work at succeeding despite obstacles, do what's right for his children, and become part of the long, proud history that is African American culture.

ACKNOWLEDGEMENTS

Great individual works are not only a reflection of the individuals who made them, but also of the many who played a key role in the outcome. We owe a debt of gratitude for the numerous and generous contributions to this literary effort. We extend sincere thanks to Dr. Wright Lassiter for his endless and valuable friendship, support and guidance; to our loving families, including our wives Ola and Melani, who continue to validate the true meaning of partnership; to Angela, an amazing sister and daughter; and to Myles and Noah, the next generation of Ivery's for whom all efforts are realized. They are both a source of inspiration for which there is no match or measure. And, to those who have taken time to read our heartfelt words, we thank you as well. It is our hope that our experiences have as much meaning in the lives of others as they have had for us.

About The Authors

Dr. Curtis L. Ivery

Curtis L. Ivery is a nationally renowned leader in urban American affairs. The author of several books and numerous articles in national newspapers and magazines, Dr. Ivery continues his quest to strengthen communities by rebuilding the family unit and the values that create and hold it together. He is the creator and driving force behind the nationally televised and highly acclaimed summits *Responding to the Crises in Urban America* and *Rebuilding Lives: Restoration, Reformation and Rehabilitation in the U.S. Criminal Justice System.*

Long recognized in his efforts to bring about social change and awareness, Ivery is the first black man appointed to the Governor's Cabinet in Arkansas as the Commissioner for the Department of Health and Human Services during the 1970s. He also is an in-demand speaker for educational and civic organizations, as well as the recipient of numerous awards including the 2005 Michiganian of the Year award from *The Detroit News.*

The son of a laborer, Dr. Ivery was taught the value of two things—family and education—and they are the cornerstone of his personal and professional platform. Recognizing that professional success begins with the role parents play in instilling the necessary characteristics and values needed to achieve it, Dr. Ivery has made it his personal mission to educate, inspire, and actively engage African American males in the parenting process.

Leading by example, Dr. Ivery, and his wife Ola, have not only made education and family a priority for their two adult children, Marcus and Angela, but also for children in the metropolitan Detroit area and around the United States through their generous and active efforts.

Marcus Ivery

Growing up the son of Curtis and Ola Ivery provided Marcus Ivery with insight into family values and an excellent template and example.

A proponent of education and strong family values, Marcus shares his commitment and expertise with several local agencies and efforts, including the National Association of Black Accountants, Detroit Rescue Mission, and Goodwill Industries Flip the Script program for young black males, and—as its president—the Curtis L. Ivery Literacy Foundation.Most importantly, he sets the example as a father to his son Myles, understanding that this is the means of creating and sustaining generational excellence in family values and connectivity.

Ivery is honored that his first published words are in partnership with his father, Dr. Curtis L. Ivery. He and his wife and son reside in the metropolitan Detroit area.

For Further Reading:

Barnes, Delonso. *Daddy Everyday: Rewriting the Black American Dad Story.* Privately printed, 2013.

Barnes, Kevin D., Sr. *Successfully Raising Young Black Men.* Dallas: Torch Legacy, 2007.

Canfield, Ken. *They Call Me Dad: The Practical Art of Effective Fathering.* New York: Howard Publishing Co., 2005.

Coles, Roberta L. and Charles Green, eds. *The Myth of the Missing Black Father.* New York: Columbia University Press, 2009.

Connor, Michael E. and Joseph L. White. *Black Fathers: An Invisible Presence in America.* Mahwah, NJ: Lawrence Erlbaum Associates, 2006.

Dobson, James C. *Bringing Up Boys.* Wheaton, IL: Tyndale House Publishers Inc., 2001.

Edin, Kathryn and Timothy Jon Nelson. *Doing the Best I Can: Fatherhood in the Inner City.* Berkeley: University of California Press, 2013.

Fiel, Jared. *Fumbling Thru Fatherhood: Lost, Unsure, Tired, Confused—It's All Good.* Greeley, CO:, ATJA Books, 2004.

Fusco, Peter J. *A Father's Guide to Raising Conservative Gentlemen: And Saving America at the Same Time.* Privately printed, 2011.

Gipson, C. *The Black Man's Guide to Parenting: 50 Ways to Be an Effective Father.* Blue Point Books, 2006.

Gustafon, Stuart and Robyn Freedman Spizman. *Questions to Bring You Closer to Dad: 100+ Conversation Starters for Fathers and Children of Any Age!* Avon, MA: Adams Media, 2007.

Green, Tara T. *A Fatherless Child: Autobiographical Perspectives on African American Men.* University of Missouri Press, 2009.

Hamer, Jennifer. *What It Means to Be Daddy: Fatherhood for Black Men Living away from Their Children.* New York: Columbia University Press, 2001.

Hass, Aaron. *The Gift of Fatherhood: How Men's Lives are Transformed by Their Children.* New York: Fireside, 1994.

Hutchinson, Earl Ofari. *Black Fatherhood: The Guide to Male Parenting.* Inglewood, CA: IMPACT!, 1992.

McGee, Micheal. *The Re-Birth of the Black Man: Rebuilding a Generation.* Woodbridge, VA: Kingdom Journey Press, 2012.

Meslane, Mpumelelo. *A Single Black Men's Guide to "Fatherhood:" The Book for Single Black Fathers.* Privately printed, 2011.

Morton, Keith Devin. *Not Superdad: How a New Dad Connected to Fatherhood Without Any Super Powers.* Privately printed, 2012.

Nielsen, Linda. *Between Fathers and Daughters: Enriching and Rebuilding Your Adult Relationship.* Nashville: Cumberland House, 2008.

Nielsen, Linda. *Embracing Your Father: How to Build the Relationship You've Always Wanted with Your Dad.* New York: McGraw-Hill, 2004.

Paschal, Angelia M. *Voices of African-American Teen Fathers: "I'm Doing What I Got to Do,"* New York: Routledge, 2006.

Pitts, Leonard. *Becoming Dad: Black Men and the Journey to Fatherhood.* Atlanta: Agate, 2006

Pruet, Kyle. *Fatherneed: Why Father Care is as Essential as Mother Care for Your Child.* New York: Broadway Books, 2001.

Roberts, Steven V. *My Father's Houses: Memoir of a Family*. New York: William Morrow, 2006.

Samuels, Jamiyl. *Pass the Torch: How a Young Black Father Challenges the "Deadbeat Dad" Stereotype.* Privately printed, 2011.

Sanders, Herman A. *Daddy, We Need You Now!: A Primer on African-American Male Socialization,* Lanham, MD: University Press of America, 1996.

Sears, Diane A. *In Search Of Fatherhood: Transcending Boundaries.* Privately printed, 2004.

Silver, April A. ed. *Be a Father to Your Child: Real Talk from Black Men on Family, Love, and Fatherhood.* Brooklyn, Soft Skull Press, 2008.

Simms, Vance. *Dear Nathan: A Young Man's Journey to Fatherhood*. Phoenix: RICHER Press, 2013.

Thomas, Etan and Nick Chiles. *Fatherhood: Rising to the Ultimate Challenge*. New York: New American Library, 2012.

Vanderpool, Joslyn Gaines and Anita Royston. *Our Black Fathers: Brave, Bold and Beautiful.* Gretna, VA: Five Sisters Publishing, 2008.

Vaughn, Greg and Fred Holmes. *Letters From Dad*. Nashville: Integrity Publishers, 2005.

Waller, Maureen. *My Baby's Father: Unmarried Parents and Paternal Responsibility.* Cornell University Press, 2002.

Willis, Andre C. *Faith of Our Fathers: African-American Men Reflect on Fatherhood.* New York: Dutton, 1996.